Hacking

The

Productivity

Break The Myths & Learn The Tricks.
Practical Hacks to Boost Productivity for
Working Professionals, Business Owners,
and Students.

Lalit Hundalani

www.lalithundalani.com

Mail: connect@lalithundalani.com

Claim Your Free Gift!

As a token of appreciation for taking out time to read my book, I would like to offer you

my E-BOOK VERSION 2.0 as a **FREE GIFT**

Pls CLICK below to claim a FREE COPY of E-BOOK VERSION 2.0

DOWNLOAD HERE or visit
http://www.lalithundalani.com/coaching

Acknowledgments

Cover Design: Mr. Mohit Ramchandani

Editing: Ms. Niraja Bandi

Table of Contents

Claim Your Free Gift! 2

Acknowledgments 3

Chapter 1 6

Introduction 6

   2 Scenarios......................................6

   What this book holds for you? 9

Chapter 2...................................12

Understanding Productivity.............12

   Defining Productivity 12

   Why Productivity? 13

Chapter 3..................................19

Breaking the Productivity Myths...........19

Chapter 4...............................25

Psychological insights on Productivity 25

Chapter 5...............................36

Produsctivity hacks for Employees & Professionals...............................36

Chapter 6................................62

Productivity hacks for Business-owners & Employers...............................62

Chapter 7 79

Productivity hacks for Students.................79

Chapter 8...............................91

Conclusion..91

Gratitude..93

About the Author 94

Happy to Help You 96

Chapter 1

Introduction

2 Scenarios

Scenario 1

Viru S B is a senior professor in one of the leading engineering colleges in India. He has been a topper all through his student life and a teacher par excellence. He is devoted to his work and utilizes every minute of the day to accomplish his tasks. The workaholism has helped him grow rather quickly, and as a result, he became the dean of his college earlier than the other senior colleagues. He is a guy obsessed with being productive and resorts to multitasking activities of another level. His quest to become most productive has given birth to some of the exceptional or rather weird habits. His eccentricities include wearing a shirt with velcro to save time on putting up the buttons, getting shaven while taking an afternoon nap, writing with both hands, and so on. He is very punctual and disciplined to the core. He is a very normal person with nothing odd in his lifestyle.

Scenario 2

RDC is a student in the same college who loves to celebrate life. He is a free-spirited person who wants to explore new things and hates sticking to a regimented schedule. He is not a workaholic and loves to have fun. He is not a multitasker and instead believes in doing one thing at a time with complete focus. He is a brilliant student, and despite devoting less time to studies, he is a college topper. In his first year at college, observing his carefree demeanor, no one expected him to be at the top of the tally. The results were quite a shocker for everyone, including his friends, who were among the laggards despite working harder.

By now, most of you would have recognized that the above two scenarios are from a famous Bollywood movie of all times-3 IDIOTS. Viru S B was the character played by actor Boman Irani, and RDC is Ranchod das chanchad, the character played by actor Aamir khan. This movie is a perfect example of storytelling using the method of weaving in powerful messages. It has plenty of them.

Now coming back to our topic, why are we quoting the movie and the above scenarios? What is the relevance? Well, the above illustrations' objective is simple. The characters stated above are in direct contrast to each other and yet successful in their ways, as they can accomplish and achieve whatever they want to. According to viru, his methods are correct, and one must utilize time efficiently to become more productive; hence, he hates people like RDC who don't have a regimented schedule. To RDC and others, Viru is suffering from OCD(Obsessive Compulsive

Disorder) and FOMO(Fear of Mission Out), and therefore, he wants to be everywhere and do multiple things simultaneously.

So, who is right, and who is wrong? Well, if we ignore the eccentric habits of Viru for a while, both are right in their way. Both of them have habits and a schedule that works best for them and enhances their productivity. The purpose of quoting this example is to show that people are different, so are their working patterns and ways to improve productivity and peak their performance. The observation is neither new nor a discovery. We all have known people in our student and work-life, how some of the students would excel in studies, sports, and other activities. In contrast, some others would have their focus areas identified clearly, which could either be academics, sports, music, play, etc.

The bottom line is that everyone is looking for ways to be successful; success can be achieved once you reach the pinnacle of your performance, and to attain peak performance; being productive is a must. The ultimate goal or destination remains the same, but the path can be different. In our objective to become productive, we sometimes fall into the trap of emulating habits of successful people, which may or may not work for us. There is nothing wrong with following successful people, but the fact remains that it is not necessary that everyone can be productive by copying the habits of Steve Jobs or Bill Gates. If Bill gates achieved success by dropping out of college, thousands were in a similar situation but ended up nowhere; we don't know about them since they are not famous. Similarly, waking up early in the morning and be most productive might not work for everyone.

What this book holds for you?

This book is an attempt to present an alternate view to achieving peak performance by breaking common myths. You can understand self, identify the ways to boost productivity, and at the end of it, find what works best for you and, more importantly, what you can stick to without drastically altering your lifestyle.

Since we understand that an individual can't increase his/her productivity in isolation if the environment is not supportive, we have dedicated separate chapters to illustrate the productivity hacks and techniques for employees/professionals, businesses/organizations & students.

Whether you are a working professional, an employee, a self-employed professional, a business owner, or a student, this book holds something for you, and you will find it relevant. Read this book only if you want to achieve peak performance in your life and currently feeling stuck.

I need some **commitments** from your side before proceeding ahead:

1.You will start taking notes as you start reading the book.

2.You will identify at least five hacks from this book, which you can adapt quickly to your lifestyle and follow consistently.

3.You will plan your schedule around these hacks.

4.Your action plan will be ready by the time you complete this book.

5.You will follow the action plan for 30 days (after which it will follow you).

6.Every time you falter, start the 30-day action plan again.

7.If you feel demotivated, reread the book.

Why these commitments?

Some of you might be thinking, why am I asking for commitments? Who asks for a commitment to read a book? Let me explain; it's because of these reasons:

1. I don't want this to be another book, which you will read but not act upon.

2.The time you will spend reading this book can be spent on any other activity. I, therefore, want

ROI (Return on Investment) on time invested by you. The ROI can be measured in terms of the favorable outcome achieved.

3.The sure way of getting work done is by fixing accountability; hence, I am making you accountable by taking the commitment.

4. The objective of writing the book is to add value to your life, and I have spent a significant time researching and writing it; hence I don't want my effort to be wasted by your inaction.

I am delighted that you have made these commitments, and I congratulate you for taking the first step.

As the saying goes, **"A Journey of Thousand miles begins with a single step."**

Let's flip the page and begin the journey.

Chapter 2
Understanding Productivity

Defining Productivity

As per the Cambridge dictionary,"*Productivity is defined as the rate at which a company or country makes goods usually judged in connection with*
the number of people and number of materials necessary to produce the goods."

It can be explained in simple terms or everyday usage as the ability to do work in a definite time frame. Therefore, when we say a person is highly productive, we refer to their ability to do more work in a defined time frame than others. However, there is a catch here. Merely limiting the definition to the ability to complete work in a time frame, we are not making the person accountable for the desired outcome. For example, a salesperson making five customer calls a day, but none of the calls is converted into an actual sale. Can you consider the salesperson as productive? If we go by the definition of productivity, he has completed five calls a day, which he was supposed to do; therefore, he should be productive. Right? Well, actually, no. The reason is accomplishing the desired outcome: The salesperson's objective is to convert the customer calls into a successful sale and generate business. If he can generate business, he is productive, else not. Making customer calls is just a process towards the realization of the objective or goal. Hence, irrespective of whether he is making two calls, five calls, or ten calls, he can only be productive based on the outcome achieved. The target number of calls would depend on his conversion ratio, which depends on his skill and ability.

Therefore, the definition of productivity can be modified as ***"the ability to accomplish a task/work towards the realization of the desired outcome in a definite time frame."***

The crucial thing here is to define an outcome before measuring productivity. If you can achieve the required result by doing work, you are productive, else not. How much hard work you put in or how many hours you dedicate may earn you an appreciation for your efforts but has no bearing on being productive unless the result is achieved. With this, we also get the clarity that being busy and being productive are not the same. However, many times both the terms are used interchangeably. In our daily lives, we assume that we are productive by working hard and keeping ourselves busy; actually, it's not true.

Why Productivity?

If we look around, we will notice that everyone is striving hard to be productive in the current scenario. Whether it's a working professional, a housewife, a business owner, or a student, all want to increase their productivity. A question may arise in our mind; why is it so?

Well, everyone has different reasons for this; let's understand this segment-wise.

Organization/Business

- **Objective**-Maximize the profits.
- **Rationale**- A higher number of productive employees will mean that a smaller number of people can do more productive work, which means a cost reduction and, therefore, higher profits.

Professionals/Employees

- **Objective**-Earning and career growth.
- **Rationale**-By being more productive, an employee can generate more revenue for the employer (either directly or indirectly), which will increase his/her worth/value in the organization. Higher value addition and contribution would mean better opportunities for earning and career growth.

Housewife

- **Objective**-Earning &/or time to pursue hobbies
- **Rationale**- For a housewife or homemaker, higher productivity means

extra hours in hand, which can be utilized towards pursuing hobbies, following a passion, or the opportunity to earn passive income.

Students

- **Objective**-Excel in academics, pursue hobbies, part-time earnings
- **Rationale**-Ability to complete more course content in less time provides an opportunity to devote time for extra-curricular activities, hobbies, or part-time work for extra earnings.

The common thread that binds together people across different segments is the intent or desire to achieve more in less time and succeed. Each of us has only 24 hours in a constant day, and howsoever hard we may try, we just can't change it. However, the utilization of this time is variable. How effectively we use these 24 hours to realize the desired outcome decides how successful we are, which is determined by our productivity levels.

Therefore, we can safely infer that productivity is a crucial metric for success, and since everyone wants to achieve success, hence the importance of productivity.

It would also be appropriate to say that higher productivity results in higher satisfaction and, therefore, happiness, while lower productivity makes you dissatisfied and grumpy. Imagine a typical workday when you could accomplish whatever you had planned; the mental satisfaction and contentment it gives can't just be explained in words. Although you would be tired otherwise, just the act of delivering the required outcome efficiently gives you a high. We can therefore summarize the productivity benefits as under:

High Productivity=HigherAchievement=Success=Work Satisfaction=Happiness

As Paul Krugman says in **_The Age of Diminishing Expectations_**,

"Productivity isn't everything, but in the long run, it is almost everything."

Chapter 2: Summary

Defining Productivity

- **Productivity** is the ability to accomplish a task/work towards realizing the desired outcome in a definite time frame.

- The outcome achieved has more relevance than the time spent or effort applied.

- Being busy and productive is not the same.

Why Productivity?

- Everyone strives to achieve more in life and therefore needs to accomplish more within the definite time available.

- **Segment-wise objectives** for high productivity:

  Organization/Business: Objective-Maximize profits.

  Professionals/Employees: Objective Earning and career growth.

  Housewife:
  Objective-Earning &/or time to pursue hobbies.

Students: Objective-Excel in academics, pursue hobbies, part-time earnings.

- **Productivity** is a crucial metric for success, and since everyone wants to achieve success, hence the importance of productivity.

- HighProductivity=HigherAchievement= Success=Work Satisfaction=Happiness.

Chapter 3

Breaking the Productivity Myths

The importance of productivity has given birth to many myths, and, in this section, we are going to break them. The myths have their origins in the conventional way of working and are now embedded in our belief system. The process of addressing these myths is something akin to the concept of unlearning to learn more.

Myth 1: Multitasking is the key to high productivity

Fact: There is almost a consensus that people who can do multiple tasks simultaneously are more efficient and can accomplish more. You will hear senior management talking about the importance of multitasking and showering praise on employees who multitask across organizations and businesses. However, researchers have shown that it is essential for better output to focus on one task and do it with full concentration. Interruptions as brief as 2-3 seconds are enough to distract the mind and increase errors. Frequent switching between tasks slows down the pace of work and hampers productivity.

Myth 2: Working in a Standing position enhances productivity

Fact: Working in a single posture, whether sitting or standing, is not suitable for health. Therefore, it is crucial to keep changing the posture regularly instead of continuous work in a single position. A combination of sitting, standing, and moving around throughout the day works best. Among other things, this variation ensures an increased flow of blood to the brain. More blood means more energy and oxygen, which helps the brain perform better and improves cognition, therefore, productivity.

Myth 3: The more hours you work, the more you get done.

Fact: Working at a stretch is detrimental to accomplishing more and adversely affects the quality of work. Taking regular breaks, enough rest, and sleep allows the mind to generate new ideas when you resume work. By devoting fewer hours to work, there are greater chances of achieving more in less time.

Myth 4: The secret to improving productivity is to find the right system and stick with it.

Fact: There is no perfect system for anything. You need to find what works for you and get on with it. Every person and every workday is different. While we may develop new strategies and habits that work for us most of the time, our jobs and lives will always throw us curve balls that lead to less-than-perfect results. We need to accept this imperfect reality, forgive ourselves, and try again tomorrow.

Myth 5: You need to be updated on what's happening around you to stay ahead.

Fact: You just need to know what's relevant to you. Information overload is just mind-boggling. Mindless internet surfing, reading multiple newspapers a day, watching the news on TV don't add any value in increasing productivity; instead, it delays the action. The key is to limit the intake of information which is relevant and act upon it immediately.

Myth 6: Micromanagement enhances the quality of work

Fact: In the short term, it may get you better results, since you can only do your work in the best possible way. But in the long run, it limits your ability to undertake more tasks and move up the ladder. Remember, we have only 24 hours in a day, and if we decide to do everything on our own, it will slow down our pace. Studies have suggested that by managing less, you can achieve more. I know many managers would be wondering, how is it possible? But the fact is backed by Science. Many people are motivated by autonomy rather than rewards or financial gains. Responsibility makes people accountable and increases ownership of work. The surplus time in your hands can be utilized for tasks of a higher caliber which only you can do.

Myth 7: You must follow the rule of Zero pending mails

Fact: The goal of zero mail in the inbox doesn't work for everyone. It tempts you to keep checking the mails throughout the day and is a significant distraction. The key is to designate specific time slots in a day for reading and responding to emails. That way, it takes less time and will let you focus on other essential jobs at hand.

Summary: Chapter 3

Myth 1: Multitasking is the key to high productivity.
Fact: Multitasking reduces focus. Monotasking increases productivity.

Myth 2: Working in a Standing position enhances productivity.
Fact: A combination of different positions like sitting, standing, and walking is preferred.

Myth 3: The more hours you work, the more you get done.
Fact: Number of hours has no bearing on your productivity. It is the focus and intensity of work that impacts results.

Myth 4: The secret to improving productivity is to find the right system and stick with it.
Fact: There is no right or perfect system; find what works for you and get going. The important thing is to act rather than procrastinate in the guise of perfection.

Myth 5: You need to be updated on what's happening around you to stay ahead.
Fact: Just focus on what you need to know. Don't aim to become an encyclopedia of a human search engine.

Myth 6: Micromanagement enhances the quality of work

Fact: It's more of a duplication of work and a waste of time. Let the people do their job, and you focus on yours.

Myth 7: You must follow the rule of Zero pending mails.

Fact: There are no rewards for nil pending emails in your inbox, so no point getting anxious. Just prioritize what's essential and attend accordingly.

Chapter 4

Psychological insights on Productivity

Most of us are aware of the benefits of high productivity and the riches it can bring to our lives. Why is it then we fail? What stops us? In this section, we will cover human psychological behavior and reasons for low productivity. With these insights, you can build a system that works best for You. As discussed earlier in the book, copying the habits or working styles of the rich, famous, and successful people may not work for all. By deep-diving into human psychology, we can arrive at a system customized for us.

The inputs are a combination of relevant areas of psychology, neuroscience and backed by numerous studies & research.

1.Role of mental health

Mental health plays a very crucial role and has a significant impact on the creativity of an individual. Negative emotions like fear, anxiety, stress, worry, depression, etc., break the chain of thoughts and interfere with your creative thinking process. If these emotions preoccupy the mind, there is a tendency to go back to the events and situations which caused these emotions. Mind also starts wondering how to get rid of these emotions, and therefore, you can't concentrate on your work. Even before completing the task, you get into self-criticism mode, analyze the output, and start giving up midway.

Researches have proved empirically that negative emotions have a destructive impact on work, and getting the right result from someone having poor mental health is just not possible. Unhappy employees can't contribute significantly to the realization of organizational goals. You may often find that organizations having toxic work cultures suffer the perils of low employee productivity and high attrition.

The way to combat it lies in creating an environment that reduces negative emotions and promotes common wellbeing. Supervisors, colleagues, and family have a vital role to play in this. The impacted individual should pro-actively reach out for support to the concerned stakeholders and seek help or guidance. You should know that fighting the lone battle with mental issues is not easy, as your ability to find solutions is lowered during this phase. The mind is so preoccupied with negative emotions that it reduces your view of life as a whole. The mind keeps looking for confirmation bias to establish the harmful codes.

As per a study, happy employees were 10-12% more productive than others. Poor mental health just squeezes out the creative juices. Therefore, ignoring mental health is a BIG NO. The more you disregard and delay addressing it, the higher will be the suffering in your personal and work life. Hence, if you focus on mental health, productivity will flow.

2.Sleep Deprivation

We all recall the days when we cannot get a good night's sleep due to an exam, an early morning flight, an important project deadline, or some exigency. Do you remember the feeling the next day? We feel irritated, face mood swings and lose the ability to do tasks in a focused way. Quality sleep is the main factor that affects the overall functioning of the brain. It is crucial to ensure smooth processing of functions related to memory, learning, attention, concentration, and thinking. Sleep is a recovery mechanism for the human body and can't be ignored.

A study done on the employees from various industries established that employees who got a total of 8 hours of sleep had the highest productivity levels. A good night's sleep increases the attention span, enhances alertness, and therefore reduces errors. If you have trouble falling asleep, get the treatment done without wasting time any further. You just can't afford to ignore this critical element to be productive.

3.Time Factor

"The work tends to expand to fill the time available for its completion"-**Parkinson's**

law. The law can be explained in simple terms as the number of hours available at your disposal decides the duration of task completion. If you have a deadline of 1 day, you can finish it in one day; if you have seven days, then the same work will continue for seven days. Some might argue about the difference in the quality of work done in 1 day or seven days; however, researches have shown it's not significant. Some variation can be there in quality, provided the excess time is utilized productively to improve the quality of work rather than delay it until the last moment.

From personal experience, I can tell you that on a majority of occasions, surplus time results in shifting the work to a lower level on the priority list and then completing it when the deadline is just around the corner. Students can primarily relate to it where the assignments are delayed indefinitely, and work starts only when the last date of submission is looming large on their heads. In fact, the late submitted project reports are, more often than not, prone to inferior quality. Irrespective of the actual deadline, give yourself less time to complete the task so that you can keep moving and engage in new activities. Needless to say, productivity will move up without you consciously noticing it.

4.I will do it all mindset

Often, we want to complete a task in the best possible way and refrain from delegating it. There is a lack of trust and fear that the quality of work will deteriorate and results will suffer by delegating. For some jobs, this approach is acceptable, and one must do what they are good at, but trying to do everything by yourself and considering you know the best of all is not the right way. This leads to a situation where one starts believing that only I can do my work and no one else can. This is what we call perfection syndrome. The fact remains that you can be good at multiple things, but you just can't be good at everything. Therefore, allowing others to do what they are good at will save you significant time.

To move up the ladder, one needs to learn the art of effective delegation; else, you can't be productive. Every time you face such a situation, just ask yourself," Is this work worth my time?". What is the opportunity cost of time invested in this task? More often than not, you will get an answer to make the decision.

5.Procrastination trap

Ideas are worthless unless executed on time. Procrastination is an extension of perfection syndrome. It's good to have a grandiose vision, a powerful mission, have noble thoughts, brilliant ideas, and a penchant for learning new skills, but everything falls flat if there is no execution. Even when you have the required skills to get the work done, preparing too much is a procrastination symptom. The primary reason for procrastination is the urge to satisfy the need for instant gratification in the present rather than working on something that will yield results in the distant future.

Human beings tend to make decisions based on their emotions and justify with logic. The actual reason for delaying the work at hand can be perceived anxiety related to task completion, but we may like to explain it with more preparation, lack of required skills, etc. The best way to address this situation is to get going and learn the additional skills (if required) as you go along. Keeping the instant gratification monkey at bay, sacrificing instant pleasures, and focusing on the bigger job at hand is essential to prevent yourself from getting into the procrastination trap.

6.I know it all bug

The condition where we prefer to continue working with our conventional methods and detest change. We believe that methods known to us are the best methods, and since they have worked for us in the past, they will continue to work in the future. There is a rigidness to learn new ways of doing things. To learn is one thing but to unlearn and relearn requires additional effort and change in mindset. A simple example can be the usage of keyboard shortcuts while using a PC or laptop. Using keyboard shortcuts inarguably saves a lot of time, and there is no disconnect on it but since learning these shortcuts requires extra effort, we prefer doing it our way.

Another example is the adoption of technology. To share a personal example, my father is still not comfortable using an ATM card for banking transactions. The card and pin process is still not very convenient to him. He prefers to visit the branch even for routine tasks like deposits and withdrawals. He is a retired person so it doesn't matter for him but for someone who can complete other stuff during the time spent in visiting the branch, the opportunity cost of time is high. If we look around, we can find many such instances.

Recently I read on a social media platform if you are in the '30s or '40s, having a mentor in the '20s is essential, and I couldn't agree more. Having a young mentor keeps you updated with changes in a fast-paced world and offers the opportunity to look at things from a fresh perspective. I remember one of my earlier bosses, who used to interact daily with a bunch of new management trainees who recently joined the organization. Initially, I couldn't understand why I used to think the new joiners should first be allowed to learn the ropes of business before we expect them to start contributing. However, my thought process was turned upside down when I could see the tools like google forms making their way into our daily business a few months later.

Upskilling is very important, and learning is a continuous process. As discussed in the section on procrastination, we can always learn while on the job; else, we may fall into the trap of procrastination and stop working altogether.
The willingness & ability to unlearn and learn is crucial to stay ahead in the productivity curve.

7.Output anxiety

Most of us either stop at nothing or want all, which leads to situations where we might just get overwhelmed by the task's enormity & lose motivation to pursue it midway. A typical example is when trying to lose weight, we shift from our usual diet, which may be around 4000 cal per day to 2000 cal per day, and then start weighing ourselves daily. Knowing fully well that we didn't pile up those inches in one day, getting rid of the excess fat will also take its own time. When we don't see the results coming through, we give up in the middle and go back to 4000 cal /day. Between 4000 and 2000 we can also limit ourselves to consuming 3000 cal/day which is more sustainable and once body get used to it we can gradually bring it down to 2500 and 2000 as the body adapts to this new way. Instead of weighing daily, measure your weight once a week so that you can see the gradual movement in scale and stay on track. We already know most of this stuff; the only problem is the application.

Imagine if a mountain climber just keeps thinking about the height they need to scale; the chances are that they would never complete it due to worry and anxiety. Even in writing, many books don't see the light of the day as authors just burden themselves by overthinking about the completion instead of enjoying the writing journey. An alternate and effective way would be to focus on today and just do what you can achieve today and keep moving. This way, we will not only be able to achieve the goal without panicking but would also be able to enjoy the entire journey. This method can also be applied to improve productivity. Instead of being overcome by emotions and deciding to do ten things a day while earlier, you may be doing just three tasks a day; aim for a small increment every day. It should be a reasonable, realistic, and tiny enough target, achievable by an average person without extraordinary effort.

A mere 1% rise in weekly productivity can improve your productivity by 80% in 1 year. A daily increment of 1% in productivity can translate to a 3900% increase in annual productivity. Do we need to say more?

Summary: Chapter 4

Psychological insights on Productivity:

1.Role of mental health: Taking care of mental wellbeing precedes physical health. Achieving high performance while negative emotions rule over your mind and dominate the thought process is challenging.

2.Sleep Deprivation: Adequate sleep is essential to recharge the brain cells and bring about the required focus. Four hours of intense work with all your faculties awake will give you much better results than 8 hours of labor in a fatigued state.

3.Time Factor: Assign a deadline to activities, as per the nature of work. Tasks without a timeline for completion never get done. If you want to do work, set a target date/time of completing it and work backward. The way the mind works will simply amaze you.

4.I will do it all mindset: Get rid of perfection alibi to delay the work. It's better to start and improve midway rather than waiting indefinitely. Perfection doesn't exist; there will always be scope for improvement.

5.Procrastination trap: Got the idea, acquired knowledge, learned the skills, but what about the application? What is the reason for the delay? Stop giving excuses and rationalizing them.

Procrastination has nipped many great ideas in the bud. Get rid of the procrastination trap by the only possible way, action.

6.I know it all bug: Learning is a continuous process; nobody knows everything. Being receptive to new ideas, skills, and knowledge enhances the learning curve. **Learning source doesn't matter; learning content does.** Being adamant in approach hurts nobody but you.

7.Output anxiety: No point getting stressed about something which you can't control. Focus on input more than the output. Instead of getting overwhelmed by looking at the required outcome, think and improve the quality of input. Your current state is an outcome of your past deeds, and your actions now will shape your future.

Chapter 5

Producstivity hacks for Employees & Professionals

This section will cover the hacks that employees and working professionals can implement in their daily routine to increase productivity. The hacks are relatively simple, but the only requirement is to be consistent with their application so that this doesn't become a one-time affair.

1.Monotasking

As per research data, productivity reduces by 40% when people switch between tasks simultaneously. In a university of London study, IQ dropped by 15 points for people engaged in multitasking activities. As per Earl K Miller, a neuroscience professor at the Massachusetts Institute of Technology (MIT)," multitasking is not humanly possible." It leads to more errors and less creativity. When you shift between the tasks during multitasking, the brain's neural networks have to go back to ascertain the leaving point and then reconfigure. This activity causes the slowdown and errors to creep in.

The solution to this problem is monotasking, which allows the brain to focus on one thing at a time and enhances creativity. Through personal experience, you would also observe that when we focus our mind on a particular item, we can think more creatively and get new ideas to accomplish the task most efficiently. The brain is like a muscle; it becomes better with use. Like in a physical workout session, focussing on single muscle yields better results; the same applies to the brain as well.

So, the first thing which one must do is to replace multitasking with monotasking. Choose an environment that encourages the ability to focus on one task at a time. Focus on small blocks of time for intense activity doesn't matter, even if it's 5-10 minutes in the beginning.

Fortunately, the more we work on focusing on one task at a time and ignoring distractions, the more we exercise the prefrontal cortex – the more evolved part of our brains. It becomes easier to focus and accomplish more.

2.Align your work as per the productivity zone

As per Eric Bloom, president and founder of Manager Mechanics LLC, our productivity levels are not the same at all hours of the day. Therefore, to maximize the output, it is crucial to identify your productivity zones. Eric has identified four zones of personal productivity:

T-Top of your game
A-Alert, but not creative
S-Sluggish

K-Keeping awake

As per the specific productivity zones, align the tasks and activities to minimize errors and complete the work faster.

The TASK process's first step requires matching the days' time zone with your productivity zones, which means understanding and establishing the body's biological clock and sync your work. Early risers are at their best during the early morning hours and therefore prefer waking up early while night owls work best during the day's ultimate hours.

Now let's look at the work and activities recommended in the TASK process:

T-Top of your game: Always reserve your **important work** for the **T zone**. During this time, you are at your mental best. All of your mental faculties are alert, awake, and ready to go. Doing creative tasks like writing, presentation, strategic planning, finalizing speech, reading, etc., are the activities that can be done during this part of the day. For most, if not all, hours at the start of the day or once you get up after sleep usually qualify for T zone.

A-Alert, but not creative—Always align your **urgent work** for the **A zone**. This phase requires accomplishing tasks, which require the moderate application of mind and doesn't require much creativity. Doing logical or analytical work, requiring the application of established methods or a repetitive task, can be done during this part of the day. Responding to emails, working on excel, data entry tasks, etc., are the recommended activities.

S-Sluggish-Do the **mundane tasks**, which require the minimal application of mind while in **S Zone**. Clearing spam folders, organizing mails, searching for presentation graphics, follow-up on the phone for pending stuff with others, preparing the to-do list are some of the recommended activities in this phase.

K-Keeping Awake- least productivity activities to be done in K zone. This is usually the time that precedes your sleep time, brain alertness is least, and focusing on essential tasks is impossible. Cleaning the surroundings, clearing the trash, organizing the files and stuff are some of the jobs which can be done before signing off for the day.

Is it possible to purposefully raise the zone, i.e., switch frosm A to T zone or K to S? The answer is a Yes and No. It depends on which time of the day we are trying to attempt it. For example, if you feel sluggish in the afternoon, external stimulants like drinking coffee or taking a walk can help you switch to an A-alert zone, but the same may not work at night (unless it's your natural T or A zone).

Don't procrastinate, do the work as per the applicable time zone, else you will have to do it in a different time zone and won't get the desired results.

3.Batching the tasks

Batching similar tasks in a single session improves productivity. As a thumb rule, we should avoid doing activities that involve the activation of both the left and right brain, as it slows down the pace of work. The right brain is in charge of the creative faculty, while the left brain is more analytical and logic-driven. Activating one part of the brain simultaneously by doing a similar kind of work ensures accomplishing more. Let's understand this with an example: writing a blog, article, or book is a creative process, and it requires activation of the right brain, hence doing such tasks in a single go saves a lot of time for us.

Taking this a step further, I would also recommend refraining from formatting and editing while writing in the process of free flow. I know it's easier said than done, but with practice, this can be achieved. Similarly, the grouping of activities like responding to calls, attending to emails, etc., during designated hours of the day.

4.Apply Rule of 3

For ages, there have been recommendations on preparing a To-do list, clearly jolting out the activities which need to be accomplished during a specific time frame. Most of the successful people have stuck to this habit throughout their lifetime and grown. However, while preparing a to-do list, it's important to remember that the purpose of preparing the plan is essentially to accomplish these tasks. Many people make the mistake of including many activities in their to-do list, which leads to confusing themselves and their brain. No wonder, most of the time, the output does not commensurate with the list prepared, leading people to question the efficacy of this activity. Lack of the desired result pushes people to give up even before it becomes a habit. The workable solution to this problem is to limit your to-do list to essential tasks only.

Chris Bailey, the accomplished author of the best seller book, **The Productivity Project**, recommends the Rule of 3, which requires an individual to identify only three tasks at the beginning of the day, which you want to accomplish by the end of the day. This activity will help you sort your to-do list and prioritize the top 3 tasks only at a time. Steve Jobs, the late co-founder of Apple, famously worked by this rule. In his team meetings, he asked the employees to come up with ideas to be focused upon to move to the next level. From the long list prepared after compiling inputs from everyone, only three points were chosen by him, which the entire team used to focus upon and deliver the results.

The Rule of 3 has been time-tested, proven, and is an effective measure of improving productivity.

5.Learn to delegate

As per dictionary meaning, "Delegation is the act of delegating or investing with authority to act for another." One of the most prominent challenges leaders face is how to delegate work effectively. It is an indispensable skill. Delegation means:

- Assigning power, authority, and tasks to others.
- Authorizing others to make decisions and implement tasks.

Therefore, from the very definition, it's clear that delegation requires the assignment of tasks and then authorizing or empowering others to make decisions. If you assign work and then continuously supervise or monitor them, it's not delegation; it's micro-management.

Delegation enables the doer to carry out tasks without your direct involvement and thereby saving your time. For effective delegation, you must stick to the following steps:

Step 1: Identify the tasks which can be delegated.
Step 2: Identify the skill set needed to perform the task effectively.
Step 3: Assign the task to a person who has the required skill set.
Step 4: Communicate the expected outcome.

Step 5: Define the authority matrix to empower decision-making.

Step 6: If the task is critical and of longer duration, then a periodic review mechanism can be fixed to gauge the progress and correct the course if required.

Trust, encouragement, and freedom comprise the essential ingredients to master the art of effective delegation.

6.Be Happy

You must have heard the quote; happiness is a state of mind; hence it's a no-brainer that a happy sense makes people more productive. A university study of optimism and performance in call centers showed that happy and optimistic people showed greater success. Happiness researcher and author Shawn Achor once asked tax managers to perform five activities a day for three weeks. He found that the experimental group with the highest scores in optimism and life satisfaction was the one tasked with engaging people positively in the social support network. The research concluded that the most direct route to happiness was providing social support to others.

A study that induced happiness in employees found that happier employees were 12% more productive than others.

This brings to a valid question-How to be Happy?

To decode this secret, let's first understand the factors which impact happiness in our lives. Martin Seligman, one of the most notable contributors in positive psychology, has summarized these factors via a simple theory called the PERMA model of wellbeing.

1.P- Positive Emotion: How often you experience positive feelings like joy, satisfaction, contentment, etc.

2.E-Engagement: How strongly do you feel engaged with people, activities, and experiences.

3.R-Relationships: The strength and quality of relationships that make you feel good and satisfied.

4.M-Meaning and Purpose: How you connect with the world, find a sense of meaning, and develop a broad vision to live a fulfilling life.

5.A-Accomplishment: How strongly you feel you have proudly accomplished something valuable and meaningful in life.

Below are some ways in which we can invite happiness into our lives:

I. **Show Gratitude**: This is the simplest of the methods and requires you to be thankful to others for what you get. One benefit of expressing gratitude is that it drives away negative emotions like guilt, envy, and sorrow, making you happy.

II. **Be Optimistic and stop overthinking:** Optimism is about being hopeful and striving to do whatever it takes to reduce suffering and expect a better tomorrow. Overthinking is the antithesis of optimism. It makes you pessimistic and pushes you down the slope of hopelessness. Focus on negative things prevents positive outcomes

III. **Social bonding**: We all have heard and read the quote," Man is a social animal." Connecting with people, therefore, is one of our basic needs, and social isolation impacts adversely. In old times, ostracizing people from the village or society was practiced as a sort of punishment. Talking to people helps us alleviate stress, cope with disasters, and mitigate feelings of loneliness.

IV. **Engagement in faith and meaningful activities**: Faith lays the core foundation of our belief system; therefore, practicing faith or religion plays an important role in uplifting our mood. However, one should follow it only if one feels engaged and upbeat. Meaningful activities would mean a passion or hobby, which makes you happy. It can be running, swimming, hiking, social service, or anything else that lets you de-stress and boost overall wellbeing.

V. **Take care of your body and self**: Happiness of mind is connected with our physical health. When we are physically fit, we feel energetic, form the right image about ourselves, and are surrounded by positive energy. Taking care of the body by doing an activity that you can perform consistently increases mental health and happiness. Walking, jogging, cycling, swimming, dancing, or any other physically engaging activity can be chosen per your preference.

7.Break and Resume

Taking regular breaks ensures that the work's monotony is broken, and you resume the work with a fresh mind. The reason behind this phenomenon is the limitation of the human brain to focus on a task for a limited duration only. Working for longer durations at a stretch on an activity, especially if it requires your creative juices to flow, reduces efficiency and impacts output quality. Various studies have been done on this subject, and it has been found that people who take consistent breaks while working are found to be more productive than their counterparts who work for longer durations in a stretch.

There are various models and techniques for implementing this process. The most famous one is the Pomodoro Technique, which works around the principle of intense work sessions of 25 minutes each, followed by 5-minute breaks. **Pomodoro** means 'a tomato' in Italian, and the technique is named after the tomato-shaped timer Francesco Cirillo used (the inventor, 1980s). The Pomodoro Technique is a popular way to increase productivity by reducing overwhelm.

Let us understand the process flow of this technique:

- Pick a timer; set it to 20 or 25 minutes.
- Spend 20-25 minutes on a task.
- Once the timer rings, stop.
- Take a break of 5 minutes (cycle 1).
- Return to another 20-25 minutes on a series of tasks.
- Take a break of 5 minutes (cycle 2).
- After four cycles, take a more extended break.

There are some other models based on a similar concept and suggest 50-minute sessions with 20-minute breaks. Ultimately, it all boils down to what works for you.

8.Stop Chasing Perfection

Perfection is a standard alibi for procrastination. Many a time, we delay the execution in the guise of perfecting the plan. More often than not, it is an excuse for delay backed by logic. Let's accept the fact that perfection doesn't exist. Anything which we do is relative and is assessed or compared with similar work for its quality. It doesn't matter how much time or energy you put into perfecting that masterpiece. There will always be someone who would come with the better version. Therefore, waiting for the perfect time, the perfect environment, and the ideal place is futile. Once you have a good resource pool available at your disposal, you should get started and get going. Once you start, you will get the motivation to finish off, and your mind will keep looking for ways and means to do it better and faster. Just a small caveat, whatever we stated above in no way implies or suggests to begin without a plan or preparation. A delicate balance between preparation and perfection needs to be maintained. We must also consider the opportunity cost of time for delaying the work.

9.Nil Meetings.

In the corporate world, meetings are necessary but also one of the primary productivity killers. In the post covid-19 era, where virtual meetings have replaced physical meetings in a big way, the problem has become even more acute. With no travel or commute time involved, back-to-back meetings are scheduled, all of which are not necessary. The meetings are essentially conducted for three broad reasons:

i.   Solve a problem

ii.   Communication of information

iii.   Felicitation or celebration

Of the three reasons, the first 2 points make up for 90%, as to why meetings are conducted and eat away into productive work hours owing to the below factors:

- Not starting in time
- Digression from the main agenda
- Continuing well beyond the stipulated timeline
- The presence of all participants is not required
- Lack of preparation before meeting
- Too many unnecessary meetings
- Impromptu meetings without adequate prior notice.

The solution to this problem is to cut down on meetings by having dedicated days for meetings so that you complete other important work on no meeting days. If it's impossible to have designated no meeting days, then at least have no meeting hours to plan and focus better.

This is one sure way of accomplishing more during office hours, which is good for the employer and employees. The leadership team and senior management of the organizations have an important role to play in implementing this.

10.Be Pro-active

Being pro-active has several advantages, the most important of them being the reduction of stress and therefore better quality of work. On most occasions, the timeline of submitting a report, finalizing a presentation, etc., is known to us well in advance; still, we tend to postpone the work till the very last day. Finishing the work towards final hours increases the stress levels, thereby restricting creativity. With the deadline looming large over our head, we rush to finish the job, compromising the output quality. Being reactive also forces and pushes into troubleshooting mode, where most of the time is spent in firefighting situations. The time so spent is usually unplanned and unallocated for and eats into productive work. This creates a domino effect, where one activity suffers due to another, so on and so forth.

The key is to foresee the situations in advance and plan beforehand. It's akin to buying an umbrella at the onset of the rainy season and using it when it rains. You don't wait for the rain to start pouring before setting out to buy one.

11.Get rid of distractions

The human brain is wired to love distractions. Scientists have found that every time we take in new information, the brain releases a flood of dopamine, the reward neurotransmitter. This is why social media is so addictive. Every new story, image, or fact stimulates the rush of dopamine, which makes us crave more. The only way to curtail this process of the brain is by limiting our exposure to distractions. The usual offenders who disrupt the flow and divert attention at the workplace are interaction with co-workers, random phone calls, scrolling through social media accounts like Twitter, Facebook, Instagram, or checking the mailbox. The process flow of restricting yourself from getting distracted requires you first to identify the causes at your workplace and then address them chronologically. If not addressed timely and effectively, the outcomes may vary from merely reducing digital workers' productivity to more severe consequences for employees engaged in critical sectors like health and aviation.

12.Fix accountability

Accountability is crucial for all, more so for freelancers and people who are working on their own. Being accountable to self is very important to ward off the temptation of procrastination. It has been well proven that accountability drives us to achieve more and progress faster. Left to our free will with no one to answer to, we tend to delay things forever. You can be accountable in 2 ways:

I.   Be accountable to yourself
II. Be accountable to a friend or family member

Out of the two methods, I prefer the second one since it also makes you self-accountable. To effectively implement this technique, you must identify the friend or family member to share your plan or goals confidently. The key lies in choosing the right person for this job, who can question you without being intimidated. Just thought of having to answer someone for not doing the work in time will push you to go on. Initially, it won't be easy, but then it will become a part of you. If required, a reward and reprimand system can also be built around the process to make you progress faster. A reward could be a free lunch, and punishment could be an email to colleagues announcing that a deadline was missed.

13. Learn to say No

It is a well-established fact that you can never be productive with too many commitments in hand. Spreading yourself too thin restricts you from realizing your full potential and justifying your work. Easy, as it may sound, most of us hesitate to say NO. You are continuously bombarded by requests from colleagues, subordinates, and bosses in the workplace, each vying for your time and attention. To stay productive and minimize stress, it is therefore vital to learn the art of saying no, politely but firmly.

Most of us shy away from saying no, to avoid disappointing the other person and spoiling the relationship. Having said this, what also holds true is that committing and then not delivering on the expected lines has a similar potential of ruining a relationship, if not more.

When the chances of spoiling a relationship are equal in both scenarios, it would be wise to be clear in your communication at the very beginning and set the correct expectations. It can lead to momentary disappointment or bitter feelings, but this works better in strengthening the relationship in the long term.

Few tips can help you in making headway and make you learn how to say No.

1.Saying No to boss/supervisor: Politely explain that your productivity will be compromised by taking on too many commitments, jeopardizing your existing obligations. If they still insist, share your project/task list with them and seek help to set the priorities. This will help you in shifting the ball from your side and reduce stress.

2.Stop being Mr.Nice: Accept the reality that you just can't make everyone around you happy. By attempting to be fair and pleasant to everyone, you only overburden yourself, and people start taking you and your time for granted. You must remember that you get paid and valued for your work, and if the work suffers, your demeanor or image takes a back seat. So, don't lose focus and exit the trap.

3.Pre-empting the request: This is applicable during a meeting or a discussion, where you can see a request coming your way when your hands are already full. It is always easy to pre-empt and make your situation clear, rather than waiting for the work to come your way and then saying NO. Sometimes, a pro-active approach of stating the number of projects in hand and the approaching deadline is sufficient to clear your position and divert a task coming your way.

4.Will get back: This technique buys you some time to re-assess your to-do list and prioritize it basis on the changed circumstances. Instead of saying an upfront no, it allows you to arrive at a rational decision by carefully considering the alternatives available. It also sends a signal to the other person that his request could not be accommodated even after careful consideration, so there must be a genuine reason behind it.

5.Taking the onus: This is a classic case of blaming yourself while appreciating the other person. It requires you to praise the idea, project, task, person, or work, stating your inability to take it up due to your limitation.

14.Measure and Monitor:"*Whatever gets measured and monitored gets done.*" Therefore, it goes without saying that to check the efficacy of various techniques to improve productivity, it is imperative to measure at regular intervals. Weekly or fortnightly monitoring of the self-productivity helps in the below ways:

- Checks the progress on implementing various techniques.
- The improvement or change drives you to stay on course.
- If something is not working out, it can be discarded.
- Shows the mirror, if you had planned but not yet implemented one or more techniques

How to measure productivity?
There are various tools available to measure productivity; however, I would suggest keeping it simple by following the below steps:

1. Before starting the productivity journey, check how much you can accomplish daily/weekly/fortnightly. (Duration to be chosen depending on the interval to be used for monitoring productivity).
2. Define and write your desired output level over the chosen period.
3. Identify the techniques you want to implement in your schedule. Start with just 1,2, or 3 strategies to start with. It's

not important how many tips or hacks you decide to apply. The key is to be consistent.
4. Measure the change at regular intervals to check the progress.
5. Introduce additional techniques once you can master the ones introduced initially, and they became a part of your habit/routine.
6. Keep repeating the above steps till you reach the desired productivity level, as define in step 2.
7. If you plan to change or modify the outcome in step 2, the entire process will be repeated.

There are many more methods and tips for boosting productivity. The hacks shared are the ones, which are easy to implement and have a proven track record of producing effective results. The long lists are usually overwhelming and tend to discourage action. It is for this reason that we have intentionally kept things simple.

Summary: Chapter 5

Productivity hacks for employees and professionals.

1.Monotasking: Quit multitasking and start monotasking by focussing on one job at a time. Toggling between multiple tasks simultaneously breaks the momentum, reduces attention span, and results in substandard work quality.

2.Align your work as per the productivity zone: Understand your productivity zone and align the work accordingly.

4 Zones of Productivity:

T-Top of your game - All important activities to be completed during this time. Creative tasks requiring the application of mind should be done during this period. Eg:-writing, presentation, strategic planning, etc.

A-Alert, but not creative-Assign urgent activities during this hour, which will push you to work.Eg:-Working on excel, data entry.

S-Sluggish- Do the mundane tasks like clearing spam folders, organizing mails, searching for presentation graphics, etc.

K-Keeping awake-All the non-important work, where the application of mind is not required, should be done during this time. E.g.: -Clearing the trash, cleaning or organizing the workspace, etc.

3.Batching the tasks: Doing similar jobs in a single batch saves time Eg: Reverting your emails in a particular hour of the day.

4.Apply Rule of 3: Instead of preparing an ambitious, long to-do list and not accomplishing anything, identify three activities that are on top of your priority list and do them.

5.Learn to delegate: If you plan to do everything yourself, you won't let yourself grow. To move up in the hierarchy, effective delegation is very much required. Allow autonomy to the people around you to develop, and **Together Everyone Achieves More (TEAM).**

6.Be Happy: A pleasant state of mind generates new ideas, makes you love your work, and creates a positive environment around you. Working in a happy state ensures that you accomplish more and thereby be more productive.

PERMA model of happiness.

P-Positive Emotion: Feelings like joy, satisfaction, contentment, etc.

E-Engagement: Engagement with people, activities, and experiences.

R-Relationships: The strength and quality of relationships that make you feel good and satisfied.

M-Meaning and Purpose: Find a sense of meaning, and develop a broad vision to live a fulfilling life.

A-Accomplishment: Feeling of accomplishing something valuable and meaningful in life.

Ways to invite happiness in our lives:

   i.   Show Gratitude
  ii.   Be Optimistic and stop overthinking
 iii.   Social bonding
  iv.   Engagement in faith and meaningful activities.
   v.   Take care of your body and self.

7.Break and Resume: Working at a stretch increases fatigue. Like HIIT (High-intensity Interval Training), HIIW (High-Intensity Interval working) is a valuable tool for increasing productivity. POMODORO technique is an effective tool for working in intervals and managing time.

8.Stop Chasing Perfection: Get started and get going rather than delaying things in the name of perfection. There will always be someone better than you, and simultaneously, you would know more than someone else. Timely action lets you achieve more than a perfect move.

9.Nil Meetings: Just like technology, meetings have been over-exploited. Meetings have become giant productivity killers. Nil meeting days/hours let you focus more, build momentum and boost productivity.

10.Be Proactive: Being reactive creates stress, while the pro-active approach increases efficiency and quality of work. Starting early and finishing off before the due date always rewards you with surplus time in hand for correction and improves work quality.

11.Get rid of distractions: Minimize the work interruptions to achieve more. Distractions, whether human, material, or technological, curtail the ability of the mind to focus. Get rid of the productivity killers, be it a talkative colleague, social media notifications, a loud and noisy environment, or an uncomfortable desk.

12.Fix accountability: Accountability pushes you to work faster and do more. With no responsibility, completion of tasks is either delayed or doesn't happen altogether.

If Self-accountability is not your cup of tea, then getting a friend or family member as an accountability partner will just do the trick for you.

13.Learn to say No: Saying, 'Yes,' in your quest to be nice to everyone does more harm than good.

A polite and well thought no at the outset is much better than an enthusiastic and thoughtless yes in the beginning, followed by a sad face later. No one likes false hope. It would be good to assess how much you already have on your plate, which needs to be accomplished before you go for that extra portion.

14.Measure and Monitor: To assess the efficacy of productivity methods, timely assessment is necessary. The results motivate you to be on track and continue with the journey to achieve more.

Chapter 6

Productivity hacks for Business-owners & Employers

In the earlier section, we enumerated the ways and methods of boosting employees' self-productivity at their level. However, there is a limit to which employees can control things at their end since external factors directly impact productivity but are not necessarily held by them. The organization's overall eco-system comprising the workplace, colleagues, management, team, work culture, etc., has a direct bearing on the employee productivity level.

Workplace productivity is vital for any business; hence, improving it rests equally with the employee and the organization. Improving it will help in business growth and profitability. Workplace productivity is essentially employee productivity since employees are the backbone of any company, and therefore it's the staff or workforce on which the success of a business depends.

This section will describe the tools, techniques, and tips that can be implemented at the organizational level to increase productivity.

1.Right Hiring

The first step and undoubtedly, the most crucial one. Faltering in hiring the right candidate has long-term repercussions; hence, hiring needs to be done with utmost care. Most organizations commit a common mistake during this process, focusing excessively on skill rather than cultural fit. Values, ethics, expectations, and goals are critical components of an organization's culture. Every company has a different work culture. The fitment of the employees within the culture is the first step that lays the foundation for a long-term association of the employee leading to higher productivity and performance.

Researches have shown that employees in sync with how the organization operates add more value, bring in more benefits, and continue for a longer duration. A combination of all these factors over the long term is a highly engaged, self-motivated, and productive workforce that can bring great results.

2.Train the employees

Once hired, training is the most crucial step. Even if the employee has the required skills, training them as per the company's requirement provides clarity and a well-defined path. Most large organizations have realized the importance of training and have dedicated teams/departments to address the employees' learning & development needs. The small and mid-level companies and even some large corporates still ignore employee training to a large extent. The result is either no training or merely a tick-in-the-box kind-off exercise.

Studies have found that training helps both employers as well as employees by improving efficiency and productivity. According to a 2013 study, the effects were observed both on new as well as existing employees. It acts as a useful tool of hand-holding and onboarding for recruits, while for existing employees, it acts as a refresher to improve productivity.

3.No micromanaging

There is nothing more painful for any employee to be conscious of the fact that he is being watched at every step. This prompts them to keep looking over the shoulder and impacts productivity adversely. According to Robby Slaughter, a productivity expert, the most effective tool for increasing team productivity is just to have the managers back off. This allows team members to take ownership of time and resources for effective utilization. It's a self-correcting, counter-intuitive process: **Manage less and get better results.**

Science also backs up the premise; most people are more strongly motivated by autonomy than financial rewards. For managers, to quit micromanaging is easier said than done. Supervisors, who excel in day to day operations of the business or owners who have started the company from scratch, have a tough time keeping their hands off it. They fall into the trap of doing things in a set pattern, which has worked for them. This creates a vicious circle, where continuous monitoring and criticism make the employees nervous; they commit mistakes, increasing supervision and monitoring. It's a never-ending unproductive loop that managers, supervisors must exit sooner than later.

Trust your employees, coach them when needed instead of doing it for them. Learn the art of letting go and allow employees to take control. It will yield twin benefits of improving employee productivity as well as managing productivity. Leaving the day-to-day operations to staff enables the managers to utilize the spare time for strategic thinking, thereby contributing more to business growth.

4.Communicate clearly

Almost every employee will agree with the adverse effects of poor communication in the workplace. Insufficient or inaccurate transfer of information diminishes workplace productivity, and in extreme situations, work doesn't happen, and goals are not met. In the absence of effective two-way communication, businesses falter.

Clear communication from the top management and leadership team ensures that the organization is headed towards a common goal. The transparency in communication fosters a sense of belongingness and provides clarity of direction to its employees. Setting clear expectations and responsibilities results in an engaged, productive workforce.

It is said that typically 80% of the work-related conversation happens around the past problems,15% concentrates on what is happening now, and only 5% on what needs to be done in the future. This is a counter-productive scenario, as 80% of the time is spent assigning the blame for wrongdoings of the past and a meager 5% discussing future possibilities.

Therefore, the first step towards ensuring clear positive communication would be to flip the script and discuss the future more than the past. The business reviews should spend less time on "why things didn't happen & fixing blames" and more on brainstorming," how to ensure achievement, as we move ahead." It's nowhere being said that one should ignore past failures. Instead, we should learn to approach situations positively.
Openness and positivity in communication set a precedent for team members at every level.

5.Encourage self-care

Employee care is more relevant in the current scenario, where work-related stress has increased multi-fold in the COVID-19 era. As per the American Institute of stress, "Occupational

pressures and fears are far and away from the leading source of stress for American adults." The situation is no different in any other part of the world. The number of employees falling sick due to work-related stress has increased multi-fold.
The excessively stressed employees are in an unhealthy state, physically, mentally, and emotionally. The motivation levels are down and zeal to achieve is non-existent; it is said that you can't win a battle with a low morale team. All in all, when you have a stressed team, everyone loses.

A run-of-the-mill organization focuses on growth, and employee care takes a backseat. Such organizations might succeed in the short term but lack a long-term vision.

While a great organization understands the importance of employee wellbeing and always puts people first. These are intelligent organizations led by visionary leaders who fully understand that they can achieve exponential growth and unique financial goals by taking care of their workforce. Frankly speaking, it doesn't take much to inculcate a healthy, communicative culture. It can very well be done by simple acts of,

- Listening to employees.
- Understanding their pain areas and addressing them.
- Ensuring constructive feedback mechanism.

- Increasing employee engagement by assigning challenging, meaningful work.
- Establishing exact parameters of success.

A happy, inspired, and motivated workforce can let you achieve extraordinary results you won't even have dreamt of. Care about your employees, and they will happily go that extra mile without you even asking for it.

6.Permit remote working

The COVID-19 crisis pushed organizations to explore remote working. Left with no other option, even conventional banking, education, schools, insurance experienced the otherwise unexplored world of remote working.

Even before the pandemic struck, numerous researches were conducted, and many exciting things were discovered about the benefits of remote working. Remote workers were more productive, performed better, put in more hours, took fewer leaves, and were generally more engaged at work. One of the crucial advantages of remote working is saving on commute time by avoiding long traffic snarls, which impact your time and take a toll on physical and mental health.

For businesses, it also results in significant cost savings towards office infrastructure and associated paraphernalia. As per the Gallup report, between 2012-2016, the number of employees working remotely jumped from 39% to 43%. Not surprisingly, organizations and businesses realize it and reaping the benefits of increased productivity and reduced cost.

The concept of remote working re-affirms that if organizations focus on the bigger picture, which is maximizing the output and reducing cost, rather than being steadfast about the conventional way of working, result turn-out is much better.

7.Better employee perks

All the great organizations realize the importance of employee perks and the resultant impact on employee morale. New age organizations like Google and Facebook are renowned for offering some out-of-the-box perks and incentives like massage rooms, nap pods, and complimentary haircuts. These organizations have realized the importance of job satisfaction, and perhaps, that's also one of the reasons they have been able to outsmart the competition. No wonder these companies count among the best places to work.

Now, you don't necessarily need to be a large organization to provide your team with extras that add to loyalty and increased morale. Simple acts of offering books, movie tickets, dinner vouchers, discount coupons, e-learning modules, subsidized gym memberships, etc., might just do the trick. Even simple perks can enrich employee lives. A recent survey by Glassdoor has also re-affirmed that 80% of employees would prefer perks to a pay raise. Need we say more and look further?

8.Improve Workplace conditions

The working environment has a crucial role to play in employee productivity. How the employees feel and are looked after in the work environment has an important bearing on employee engagement. Some of the aspects of the work environment include,

1. **How well lit the environment is**: You just can't expect employees to be at their best in a dull, gloomy environment; that's entirely counter-productive. Whether natural or artificial, the availability of a good light source is the first and foremost for creating a positive work environment.

2. **Temperature & cooling**: Extreme temperature conditions don't augur well for people spending long hours in the office. Hence right temperature and cooling conditions are essential to avoid distraction and boost productivity.

3. **Common area and facilities**: The availability, upkeep, and condition of common area facilities like toilets, pantry, canteen is an indirect way of showing how much you care for your employees. More-importantly non-availability of these facilities within the work environment requires employees to venture out, which

is an inconvenience and results in the loss of productive work hours.

4. **Cleanliness & hygiene**: This aspect has a direct impact on employee health and wellbeing. So, if you don't want your people to fall sick, you must take care of cleanliness and hygiene. Remember, a sick employee also results in the loss of productive working hours.

5. **Work station ergonomics**: This refers to the desk arrangement whereby employees can work efficiently without much distraction.

6. **Availability of quiet spaces to focus**: Open workspaces are intended to increase collaboration and encourage positive relationships between team members. However, the flip side of this setup is chaos. We all can recall the incessant talker, the phone shouter, or that food lover who just relishes devouring that massive meal at the desk. It isn't easy to concentrate in such an environment, especially if you have an important project at hand. Setting up standard rooms or meeting rooms that can be utilized on a need basis may help address it without any additional cost.

9. Limit the meetings

According to a 2018 survey of employees in the UK, Germany, and France, an average staff spent close to 187 hours or 23 days in meetings. 56% of the employees were found to be unproductive by attending conferences, and 66% of the employees confessed that they made excuses to avoid meetings.

In the background of these findings, it's surprising to see organizations and managers' love affair with meetings at the cost of employee productivity. Inviting all and sundry to discussions on the pretext of employee engagement doesn't make sense. On the contrary, higher frequency and longer duration of the meetings make employees anxious about the work, which is delayed due to the meeting. This leads to reduced engagement, which is also evident from the survey findings, as stated above.

The solutions are pretty simple, straightforward, and can be arrived at by answering the below questions:

- Is it indispensable to call the meeting? Can the objective be accomplished by email, phone, or via a web-based panel?
- Does it require a contribution from all the attendees? If not, why is their presence required?
- If it's a pre-scheduled meeting, has there been enough progress after the last one?
- Is this another meeting for the sake of it?
- What is the mechanism of tracking the outcomes?
- Is the event flow defined? Has the communication gone to participants to

come with preparation, and precious time can be saved?
- Have you assigned the responsibility to someone to ensure that the meeting is on track and there is no digression from the agenda?
- What is the plan to ensure that it doesn't overshoot the defined timeline?

Once the answers to all these questions are in place, it would be easier to cut down on unnecessary meetings, and the necessary ones can be concluded in time.

10.Set Smart Goals

It's a no-brainer that high workloads and unrealistic deadlines are the most significant and common reasons for increased stress at the workplace. Therefore, setting SMART goals is a simple solution. SMART, as we already know, stands for:

S-Specific

M-Measurable

A-Achievable

R-Realistic

T-Time bound

The fastest way to disengage your employees is to keep telling them that they are not doing enough. Rest assured, soon; they will stop striving to achieve the goal altogether, which is not a good situation for an organization. Managers and businesses must understand the difference between ambitious and unattainable goals. Ambitious goals push the team, but impossible goals force the teams to give up without giving a chase. Sadly enough, some business leaders continue to stay in fools' paradise and believe that unrealistic goals push the teams and get results. In reality, this leads to a despondent workforce, poor employee wellbeing, high attrition, and ultimately poor performance.

It won't require a herculean task for a business or organization to implement the methods stated above. The techniques are relatively simple; the only prerequisite is to realize the relationship between business productivity and a happy, motivated workforce.

Summary: Chapter 6

The productivity-enhancing techniques for employers & business owners:

1.Right Hiring: Assessing the employees' cultural fit is more important than knowledge, experience, and technical skills. Hire employees who have the tenacity to continue for a longer duration and become an asset to the organization. It is a proven way to reduce employee turnover.

2.Train the Employees: Employees are the most prominent brand ambassadors for any organization. Training ensures the staff is confident and well-versed in the product/service and their role. Knowing what needs to be done and how it needs to be done accelerates the pace and quality of work, thereby productivity. An intelligent team of well-trained people can accomplish much more.

3.No Micromanaging: Define the outcome, provide the structure, communicate clearly what is expected, how it needs to be done (if necessary), assign the timeline, and back off. Let people complete things at their own pace. Micro-managing increases the duplication of work. As a supervisor or owner, you can devote the time thus saved in doing something more meaningful, which only you can do; when everyone does what they are supposed to do, the overall productivity increases.

4.Communicate Clearly: The clarity and transparency in communication fosters a sense of belongingness and clarifies direction to its employees. Setting clear expectations and responsibilities result in an engaged and productive workforce.

5.Encourage self-care: Caring about employees is what differentiates a great organization from the ordinary one.
An ordinary organization or leader would say, "Our top priority is to achieve x amount of financial growth, and yes, we do care about our employees. "

A great organization or leader would say," Our topmost priority is our people, we care about our employees, and we know if we care well enough, we can achieve extraordinary financial goals."

Putting people first and caring for them is a proven method by which people can achieve more.

6.Permit remote working: Shift the focus from the number of hours spent at work to the actual outcome achieved. Remote working or work from home offers many advantages in saving cost, time, and higher employee productivity.

7.Better employee perks: We all are aware of the carrot and stick approach for motivation. There is no dearth of stick holders at the workplace to get the work done, but carrot is mostly forgotten. Perks are the carrots, which motivate the employees to strive and achieve more. Simple acts of offering books, movie tickets, dinner vouchers, discount coupons, e-learning modules, subsidized gym memberships, etc., might just do the trick.

8.Improve Workplace conditions

1. **Well-lit environment**: Availability of a good light source, whether natural or artificial, is the first and foremost for creating a positive work environment.
2. **Temperature & cooling**: Right temperature and cooling conditions are essential to avoid distraction and boost productivity.
3. **Common area and facilities**: The availability, upkeep, and condition of common area facilities like toilets, pantry, canteen, etc. is an indirect way of showing how much you care for your employees
4. **Cleanliness & hygiene**: This aspect has a direct impact on employee health and wellbeing.
5. **Work station ergonomics**: This refers to the desk arrangement whereby employees can work efficiently without much distraction.
6. **Availability of quiet spaces to focus**: In a noisy environment, it's difficult to concentrate. Setting up standard rooms or meeting rooms may help in addressing it without any additional cost.

9.Limit the meetings: Cutting down on unnecessary meetings and concluding the necessary ones on time allows people to do more. Frequent meetings, the high number of participants, and sessions that stretch well beyond the timelines do more harm than good,

10.Set Smart Goals: SMART goals drive the team to achieve more. Unrealistic goals might look good on paper but do no good. If you want the people to do more, give them something which looks achievable. Having a plan in sight pushes everyone to walk that extra mile.

Chapter 7

Productivity hacks for Students

In the last two chapters, we covered how employees and employers can achieve more by applying simple productivity-boosting techniques. This particular chapter is devoted to the student community. I can still recall my student days when we used to be hard-pressed for time, especially during the days preceding exams. However, since the internet was yet to intrude in our lives and life was relatively simple, we were fortunate enough. I could recall few distractions, including television, playtime with friends, unannounced arrival of relatives, and family functions. Fast forward to today's information & technology age, and there are so many things to be managed. Studies, extra-curricular activities, social media, television,24X7 content streaming from OTT platforms, mobile phones, and what not.

Considering all the aforesaid reasons, it would be unfair not to share productivity hacks for students.

My sincere advice to all the student friends would be to apply these tips in their lives and see the results coming through. The only pre-requisite would be to make special efforts and remain consistent for the first 30 days, after which it will become a habit.

1.Manage yourself to manage time

Managing time is the first and most essential step towards increasing productivity. Considering the plethora of activities and tasks requiring time and attention, it's impossible to cope without setting up a priority list. Identify what you need to accomplish and prepare a checklist accordingly. One needs to have a set time to do all the stuff they have on their list for the day. Setting out specific times for specific activities helps organize the day in a much better way, rather than managing the stuff as it comes your way. It's a digital age; hence there is no scarcity of mobile applications, which can help manage and track time. Planning and tracking will help you identify the time wasters, organize yourself much more effectively, and enforce the habits of discipline and punctuality.

2.Fix deadlines

Assigning a deadline for a task creates urgency, forces the brain to work backward and find ways to accomplish it faster. The absence of a deadline is akin to a ship sailing towards the destination with no arrival timeline. For humans, it allows the mind to wander and get attracted to distractions. Without a set timeline for completion, an assignment will never be there on your priority list, and chances are you won't even start working on it. On the contrary, fixing a completion date as soon as the work is assigned will reduce procrastination and increase work efficiency. Completing work before the actual date of submission also impacts the quality of work since it helps minimize errors. Positive pressure will push you to complete it faster, provide enough time for revision, and avoid the last-minute rush, which usually leads to a mediocre job.

Inculcating this habit also prepares for work-life where there is usually a mismatch in the work to be done and time available.

3.Take Regular breaks

As stated in one of the earlier sections, scientific studies have proved that engaging the brain in a single activity for long stretches reduces the output. It's a myth that studying for long hours gets better results. On the contrary, looking for hours without a break leads to brain fatigue, and the absorption capacity goes down. There are fair chances that points might not be registered correctly. Like any other body muscle, overworking the brain without timely breaks doesn't yield the desired outcome. Pre-planned time breaks allow the brain to relax, recover and increase productivity. Some examples of study breaks include a short nap of 30 minutes, a stroll or walk for 10-15 minutes, music break, chatting with friends or family members, or any such activity that refreshes the mind. I would personally recommend choosing something which you love doing and recharge yourself instantly.

4.Batching

Grouping and executing tasks in one batch consumes less time. For example, work related to memorizing and analyzing can be performed simultaneously, while the activities related to creative writing should be performed separately. Diverse activities require the usage of different parts of the brain; therefore, aligning the work which requires activation of one half of the brain at one point in time is highly recommended. Overlapping activities that demand the left and right brain simultaneously is a complete no since switching the left, and right brain increases the processing time. It is due to this reason that batching reduces the time taken for the completion of work.

5.Recharge & Recover

"A healthy mind resides in a healthy body." This quote beautifully sums up the importance of health for the body and mind. Diet is fuel for both body and mind. Most of us know that for a healthy body, diet and exercise are essential. Interestingly, the results are governed 80% by nutrition and only 20% by training—like for a healthy body, eating the right food is crucial for developing a healthy brain and efficient functioning.

As the saying goes, you are what you eat. Eating a balanced diet comprising of macronutrients-proteins, carbs and fats is therefore highly recommended. Fresh fruits, vegetables, dairy products, and other edibles rich in essential nutrients, minerals, and vitamins ensure the body's proper functioning and avoid frequent fatigue. Processed food and unhealthy snacking should be strictly avoided as it is neither good for the body nor for the brain's healthy functioning.

A healthy diet must be backed by a healthy sleeping cycle for excellent results. Rest and recovery are essential for increasing productivity. It's common to notice, students binge-watching shows on TV or mobile platforms till late in the night and then waking up late in the mornings. Lack of sleep or a low sleeping cycle results in fatigue and reduces concentration, decreasing overall efficiency.

6.Plan your day

A routine is a pattern of doing things. Creating a routine means allocating time blocks for doing mundane activities during the day. A schedule can include wake-up time, exercise time, time for academics, pursuing hobbies, socializing entertainment, etc. With easy access to 24X7 entertainment, it's elementary to give in to temptations at the cost of a good night's sleep. As stated earlier, all these activities (including entertainment) are part of life, and a complete absistence is not possible; hence we are not recommending it either. A mix of fun and entertainment activities is also vital for refreshment and recreation. The next best way is to create a daily/weekly schedule and incorporate all the critical activities. A practical routine would include balancing work and fun activities with regular breaks interspersed in between.

7.Set Goals

Goal setting is essential for getting a sense of direction and keeping yourself motivated. Whether it's academics, sports, a hobby, a dream job, or a career, setting a goal is essential to define a purpose behind doing any activity. What is the outcome you would achieve?

For academics, it could be first-class grades; in sports, it can be securing a place in the school/college team or if you are already a part of the team, then winning the tournament or becoming the best player, if you are running a marathon than it could be the timing goal, etc. There is only one caveat that you must realize the difference between a goal and wishful thinking. Setting realistic goals and achievable goals is the key. As already mentioned in the earlier section, goals should be SMART (Specific, Measurable,

Attainable, Relevant & Time-bound). Setting unrealistic goals doesn't help, and more often than not, you give up soon after starting.

I would suggest you to go a step further and break each goal into smaller sub-goals. For example, if your goal is to lose 10 kg of weight in 10 weeks, then the sub-goals can be:

- Daily 1 hour work out
- Daily cut down on 1000 calories
- Loosing 1 kg (2.20 lbs) of weight every week

It would be best to celebrate each sub-goal realization to give you enough motivation to keep moving towards the final goal. Consistency is the key, and the achievement of smaller goals is a way to provide evidence to the brain that you are moving closer to your outcome.

Another way to keep off from digressing is by building a consequence management system, where you get rewarded for accomplishment and punished otherwise. Continuing with the above example of weight loss, you can reward yourself with a dessert or a meal of your choice once you have lost the required amount of weight at the end of week one. If you don't, you will have to skip one meal or fast for a day. The system of consequences management can be implemented either on your own if you have strong willpower, or otherwise, you can get a friend or family member to become an accountability partner. You can share your goal and sub-goals with your partner so that you are accountable to them for achievement and progress faster.

8.Find your work zone

This might sound trivial, but an important aspect nonetheless. Carefully choosing your workplace makes a big difference in the output. Distractions like overcrowding, loud music, television, noisy common areas, etc., reduce the focus and delay work pace.
The solution is to find your quiet zone so that you can finish the work faster. If you are staying at a place where privacy is unattainable, then gadgets like noise-canceling headphones may save the day for you.

9.Begin with heavy lifting

It merely means that the tasks which are going to take a long time and require maximum effort should be done in the beginning when your mind is fresh and energy levels are high. The activities requiring less effort can be done during the later part of the day when the fatigue creeps in. This sequence will ensure that you can tick off most items from your to-do list. Tackling the most challenging and least enjoyable tasks first will let you breeze through the rest of the day.

10.Take Social Media Break

Studies have suggested that social media does more harm than good. It lets people compare themselves with others basis the likes, comments, and views on social media and creates stress. Somewhere it induces a feeling of being less popular and being not good enough.

Every time you get a message and look at your phone, your mind is distracted, and getting back to your zone takes time and impacts productivity. Think of all the time wasted by checking the phone every few minutes.

This is unrequired stress and can be addressed via simple techniques like **disabling push notifications** for applications like Facebook, WhatsApp, etc. The extreme step would include **temporarily disabling the social media accounts,** or better enough, **uninstall the mobile applications** temporarily.

Summary: Chapter 7

Productivity hacks for students:

1. **Manage yourself to manage time:** Identify what you need to accomplish and prepare a checklist accordingly. Set a time for all the activities which need to be done during the day and complete them one at a time.

2. **Fix deadlines:** Assign a deadline for a task to create urgency. The brain will work backward and find ways to accomplish it faster. The absence of a deadline is akin to a ship sailing towards the destination with no arrival timeline.

3. **Take Regular Breaks:** Work in intervals to apply the principle of rest and recovery. Work intensely for the defined time frame, take a short break and resume again.

4. **Batching:** Group the tasks of a similar nature to work faster. It lets you do more and improve work quality.

5. **Recharge & Recover:** Nutrition and sleep are critical for the healthy functioning of the body and mind. Be mindful of what you eat and how much you eat. Nothing energizes you like a well-balanced diet and adequate sleep to achieve more.

6. **Plan your day:** Create a routine to allocate time blocks for activities during the day. A pattern can include wake-up time, exercise time, time for academics, pursuing hobbies, socializing entertainment, etc. The conventional method of preparing and writing down a timetable still works.

7. **Set Goals:** Decide on the outcome and work backward. Goal setting is essential for getting a sense of direction and keeping yourself motivated. Whether it's academics, sports, a hobby, a dream job, or a career, setting a goal is essential to define a purpose behind doing any activity.

8. **Find your work zone:** Identify the place where your productivity peaks and make it your work zone. The work environment has a profound impact on your productivity, so choose it carefully and stick around for consistent results

9. **Begin with heavy-lifting:** Do the most formidable task when you are in your best state. For most people beginning of the day is the time when energy levels are at their peak. Plan your day accordingly, and achieve more in less time.

10. **Take Social Media Break:** Distractions delay the pace of work, especially when engaged in something urgent or important. Mobile and social media are the flagbearers of

regular distractions. To gain speed and carry on the momentum, take frequent breaks from social media. Get off from social media for specific durations by uninstalling the applications or turning off the notifications.

Chapter 8

Conclusion

In the preceding part of the book, we understood the importance of productivity in all areas of our life. We learned how seemingly simple techniques could help us do more, achieve more, and be more productive.

All efforts have been made to keep the book concise and to the point. I am sure that you have acquired the required knowledge for being productive and attain peak performance by now.

Knowing is good, but it's the application of knowledge, which brings about the actual results. That's the real purpose and intent of writing this book. If you recall, I had asked for specific commitments from you before moving ahead. The idea was to put you into action mode right from the beginning. I understand that owing to inertia, sometimes, it takes more time to start with the action plan. If you were waiting to complete the book before starting, I would strongly urge you to get going now. Righteous people don't like to fail on commitments, and I know you are certainly not the one to falter. So, here is the action plan for you:

Action plan

1.Having gone through all the chapters, chalk out a blueprint for yourself basis your lifestyle.

2.Refer to chapter 5, chapter 6, and chapter 7 to identify your segment.

3. If you don't fit into any of the categories defined in the chapters above, pls choose the tips that relate more to you and can be easily applied in your routine.

4.Start with the application of a maximum of five techniques till you achieve consistency.

5.Start with tips that are easier to follow, so you don't give up initially.

6.Start as soon as you finish the book and measure improvement at the end of every seven days.

7.Share your plan with a friend, colleague, business partner, or family member and request them to become an accountability partner. At the end of each week, discuss the progress with them.

8.At the successful completion of each week, reward yourself.

9.Repeat the process consistently for 30 days till it becomes a habit.

Wishing you all the success on this journey to be more productive and achieve peak performance.

Cheers

Gratitude

Dear Reader

Pls, accept my heartfelt compliments and sincere gratitude for taking out your precious time to read this book. I hope you would have found the content to be useful for you. I expect that you are going to apply the learnings, knowledge & techniques to transform your life.

Feedback is very critical for continuous improvement and getting better at things. For an author, reviews constitute an integral part of the feedback mechanism. It encourages and pushes to perform better. I, therefore, look forward to an **honest review** from your end on www.Amazon.com

It will just take **60 seconds** for you but will mean a lot to me. It will help me reach out to more readers and work on your suggestions in the next book.

Thanks for your support and patience. I am looking forward to your review on https://www.amazon.com/dp/B08RWVKC9P/

Thanks

Lalit Hundalani

About the Author

Hello friends, my name is **Lalit Hundalani**. I am India's leading **Life transformation coach, Productivity Hacker, Mentor, Best Selling Author,** and **Ex-Banker**. I am on a mission to help 1 Million individuals transform their lives.

I am a certified professional in Leadership & Strategic management from the prestigious Indian Institute of Management Lucknow (IIML). I have rich experience working in the corporate sector for more than 18 years, primarily in banking and financial services. I had the privilege of working with some of the most well-known organizations, led by extraordinary leaders who played a crucial role in shaping me as an individual both at a personal and professional level.

During my corporate career, I got the opportunity to mentor and nurture incredible individuals and see them transform into successful professionals. The sheer joy of witnessing people getting their transformation was unparalleled. It also made me realize the importance of giving back to society. With this objective in mind, I decided to reach out to the people beyond my workplace and share my experience, knowledge, and skills.

Having witnessed scores of people getting their breakthroughs, I observed that on most occasions, it's our conflict with the self, which holds us back and halts the progress. We keep on looking for the reasons outside but ignore the inner-self. Once we can fix the inner self, the rest of the journey becomes a cakewalk.

I decided to delve deeper into the subject, surrendered myself to the experts in the arena, and got some path-breaking insights.

I went through the learning process and got myself certified in transformational coaching to share my learning with others. Currently, I am a practicing, **Life Transformation Coach** on a mission to help 1 Million individuals transform their lives.

I published my first book in Jan 2021 and became the author of the Amazon Best-Seller book, "**Hacking The Productivity.**" The book is a power-packed action plan to boost human productivity and achieve more in life. It has some cools hacks, which work.

I am an avid blogger, You tuber, and fitness enthusiast. I would love to connect with you and take this association forward.

For more details, you can visit my website www.lalithundalani.com

Happy to Help You

Are you an **AMBITIOUS** person who wants to make it **BIG** and lead an **EXTRA-ORDINARY** life?

Are you feeling **STUCK** and looking for help?

If, yes then read on to know how I can help you unleash your true potential and become **UNSTOPPABLE**.

VERSION 2.0 is a holistic self-transformation program that works deep in your personality and helps you overcome the obstructions to become unstoppable.

It's a proven method, which gets you clarity on:

What should you do?

Why should you do?

How should you do?

Once you get the answers to the above questions, you transform into a better version of yourself. Being consistently better every time will invariably make you the best.

Key Result Areas where this program works :

- Personal Growth
- Career
- Finance
- Health
- Relationship

The only commitment I would require from your end is **ACTION**.

Let's connect once you are ready to **ACT.**

To know more, book your FREE Session here>><u>Clarity Session</u>
Or
visit **<u>www.lalithundalani.com/Coaching</u>** to book it online.

See you soon.

Preview of another book in Self-Transformation Series

"Focus Your Way To Fortune"

Introduction

The Story of Five Sages

Once upon a time, there was a village in a faraway place. The inhabitants had easy-going life with abundance all around. However, no one visited the town for two reasons:

1. *The village was located in a far-off valley among the mountains.*
2. *The way to reach the place was long and tedious.*

Many people came to know about the prosperity and the abundance of the place. They tried reaching there but gave up once they learned about the hurdles involved in the journey.

There was an old and wise sage in the village who was the source of spiritual and moral guidance. The villagers respected him greatly for his wisdom, knowledge, and selfless service to the entire town. Sage was also very fond of the villagers, and that's why he had settled there for many years.

As he was getting older, he thought of succession planning so that people have someone to look up to, even after he has gone. Also, being a wise person, he wanted to pass the beacon of enlightenment well in time. With these thoughts in mind, he sent a message to the ashram where he originally came from.

The message was short," I am old, send one sage to whom I will transfer my learnings. Pls, ensure to send someone, mindful of distractions!"

Once the head sage received the message at the ashram, he called together all his disciples and informed them about the news. He further said that" I would like to send five of you to the village; who would like to go?" The disciples were slightly confused, and they asked why five of us when the message is for sending only one.

The head sage calmly replied, "The way to the village is long and tedious, and I am not sure that even after sending five of you, how many of you would be finally able to make it. So, I don't want to take any chances."

The young disciples were confident and argued that they were competent enough to complete the journey and reach their destination. There was no need to send five; one was sufficient. They tried to convince the head, but he insisted and finally pushed through his idea, much to the displeasure of his disciples. Finally, five sages came forward to embark on the journey. They got the necessary instructions before starting off.

Soon after starting the journey, they reached a village where they were welcomed by the villagers wholeheartedly. The people of that village were generally good and kind-hearted. Later, they realized that the village head priest had passed away recently, and the villagers were looking for someone who could fill that position. They were willing to pay the sage who would stay back to fill in the shoes of the dead priest. It was a significant amount with perks like own house, domestic help, and support for daily necessities. One of the sages was attracted to the offer and decided to stay back. He reasoned to his colleagues that the villagers needed a spiritual guide, and being on the same path, it was his moral responsibility to help them.

The other four sages tried convincing him, but it didn't work. So, leaving him behind other four continued on their journey. The fifth one stayed back in the village with a lovely home, good food, and other riches, strictly not meant for a sage.

As the four sages moved on, they reached the outskirts of a kingdom. Incidentally, the king was passing by on his horse. The king invited the four sages to his camp for food and offered them the night stay as it was already dusk. The king was generous, and he spent time during the night listening to their stories and background.

Late into the night, the sages asked for leave so that they can go back to sleep and resume their journey the next day. As they were leaving, the king asked the youngest one to stay around for a while. When they were alone, the king told him that he was very impressed by his personality, thoughts, background, and journey. He requested him to marry his daughter, stay back in his kingdom to be his successor, and become the king when the time comes. The young sage was overwhelmed by the offer as he was not expecting any such thing. He thought that if God has given this opportunity to him, there must be some reason behind it.

In the morning, he shared last night's discussion with his three friends. He also communicated to them his decision to accept the offer. Eventually, he stayed back in the kingdom to marry the princess and became the heir apparent. After that, three sages resumed their journey.

The three sages now realized what head sage was talking about and why he insisted on sending five of them instead of one. To break the trend, they made a pact to be more vigilant. They agreed to keep a watch on each other to avoid the repetition of similar instances.

As they continued on the journey, a fierce storm broke through. They mutually decided to find a safe house to weather the storm and continue the trip once it was over. They came across a place owned by a widow lady. They requested her to allow them the shelter. She was a very kind lady, who welcomed them wholeheartedly, prepared warm meals, and arranged beds to rest.

Owing to the weather and fatigue, one of the sages fell sick. The woman requested the two friends to stay back until their friend recovered. Left with no other option and not willing to leave their friend behind, they stayed back.

The lady served three of them with all the dedication and attention. She took great care of the sick sage to ensure a fast recovery. After some days, he got better and regained his health. Three sages got together and discussed the plan to continue on their journey. The sage who had recovered recently confessed that he was very impressed by the selfless service of the landlady. He was in love with her and wanted to be with her for the rest of his life. The two tried to convince him that she was just a distraction, but the smitten sage was in no mood to listen. Realizing that convincing him was turning out to be a futile exercise, they left the house and continued further. They discussed how easily their companions were distracted from the ultimate objective. They boasted about their commitment and loyalty to the task at hand.

One day when two of them were passing by a village, suddenly a crowd surrounded them. The villagers were atheists and challenged the two sages for religious debate. One of the sages got passionate and started defending the religion. He tried desperately to win the crowd with his knowledge and wits. On the other hand, the villagers were egoistic who held great pride in their knowledge and wisdom. Not the one to take things lying down, they vehemently countered all his arguments. The debate continued for several days. Finally, with no end in sight, other sage decided that it was time to carry on. He reasoned with his friend to leave the villagers with their beliefs, as the debate was not good for them. The sage engaged in the discussion disagreed and said he would go only after proving his point to the villagers, forcing them to change their mindset and convincing them to accept his religion.

It was disheartening for his friend. He tried several times and made numerous attempts, but the other sage didn't buzz. Finally, the last sage decided to continue his journey. Within a couple of days, eventually, he reached the destination. He met the old sage and communicated his availability to start the training. The old sage asked him about his journey, and the young disciple shared the details and brought him up to date with all the happenings.

After listening carefully, the old sage smiled and said, "I see the head sage deciphered my message accurately. You see, my dear young fellow, the path to this village is not that tough, but it is full of distractions. And what we as a village have managed to achieve is not that hard to achieve. But, as you have learned on your path getting here, the secret to achieving results is to be mindful of distractions. And with that, my dear friend, we have concluded your first lesson."

Moral of the Story

It's an old story, and you might have known it earlier, but the story's moral is very much relevant in the contemporary world. We may plan to achieve great things and set elaborate goals, but things don't happen if we are not mindful of distractions. Therefore, unwavering focus on the end goal and competency to avoid distractions is a must for achieving what we want.

The story signifies the importance of focus since ancient times. These were the times when distractions were limited. However, in modern times the elements seeking your attention are unlimited. In such a scenario, focus has become the most crucial skill of modern times. Mastering this one skill paves the pathway to learning all other skills. It is the essential skill that can guide us through the maze of life—the master key which can unlock many doors, provide clarity and make the journey easier.

I have personally experienced the power of focus in my life. I have felt the highs when it's present and lows when it's not. Being an author and a transformation coach, a significant part of my work requires creativity, which is impossible if the focus is missing.

There was a time when it was extremely tough for me to concentrate. I struggled a lot to focus on my studies during my school days. The slightest of noise and disturbances were enough to put me off.

I would sit for hours going through the books, but the progress was plodding. I could see others devoting less time yet finishing the tasks much faster, but it required long hours for me.

Having grown in an era where the number of hours put in signified your efforts, showed your dedication, hard work, and commitment, observing others working less and achieving more was astounding. I justified that maybe these guys were talented, more intelligent, and gifted than I am. God has been partial to me, and I can't do much about it. Like most occasions, conveniently, I passed on the blame to an external force, and life carried on. In this case, it was GOD, completely unchallengeable and unapproachable.

Soon I started noticing that it was not just 1 or 2 students, but even some of my close friends and few cousins had this ability. So, I was intrigued; how is it possible?

As I grew up, I also came across the stories of successful individuals, school & college drop-outs making it big, achieving success, and creating enormous wealth.

At the global level, the success stories of personalities like Bill Gates (Microsoft), Paul Allen (Microsoft), Michael Dell (Dell Computers),

Mark Zuckerberg (Facebook), Steve Jobs (Apple), Jack Dorsey (Twitter), Jan Koum (What's app) were the talk of the town.

Closer home, there were people like Azim Premji (Wipro), Dhirubhai Ambani(Reliance Group), Mukesh Jagtiani(Landmark Group), Sachin Tendulkar(Sports-Cricket), Aamir Khan(Movie star). They created ripples by achieving massive success in their respective fields without completing a formal college education.

This broke another notion that completing formal education is very important to become successful in life. It was not. It became more puzzling for me.

Earlier it was one question, now there were many:

- Why is it that sometimes it becomes easier for us to do a task while at other times, the same activity stretches indefinitely?
- How is it that some people work less but still accomplish more in less time?
- How is it that someone who has not completed formal education becomes super successful while the one with good grades and degrees continues to slog?
- What differentiates a successful person from an ordinary one?
- What is the most critical thing which helps in the creation of a fortune?

The quest to find the answers continued till I found that all these questions had a common thread, which was indeed the answer to all these questions.

The answer was **FOCUS**.

- ✓ When we are focused and concentrated on our job, we can accomplish it much faster.
- ✓ People with high focus skills accomplish more in less time.
- ✓ Single-minded, unwavering focus on their goals allowed school & college drop-outs to achieve massive success.
- ✓ The vagaries of life can distract an ordinary person but not the focussed one. Like the story of 5 sages, one who can cut through distractions is the one who reaches his destination.

Focus is what leads to the creation of a **Fortune.**

Why should you read this book?

The book broadly covers all the critical aspects of focus, its importance, and its role in paving the path to success. Having read this book, you will get clarity on the below points:

- ✓ What is Focus?
- ✓ How can it help in the creation of fortune?
- ✓ What is the relevance of focus in the modern world?
- ✓ What is the importance of focus in day-to-day life?

- ✓ Why do we need to focus on our life?
- ✓ Why is it difficult to focus?
- ✓ What are the various factors impacting focus?
- ✓ How can we master the focus?
- ✓ How to train our minds for focus?
- ✓ How to train our body?
- ✓ How to manage the external environment?
- ✓ 10 Step Focus to Fortune blueprint
- ✓ Bonus hacks to sharpen the focus

--End of Preview—

Get your copy of the complete book >><u>Focus Your Way To Fortune</u> on www.Amazon.com

---

References

https://www.ventureharbour.com/scientific-studies-productivity-secrets/

https://www.nytimes.com/guides/business/how-to-improve-your-productivity-at-work

https://cognitiontoday.com/how-to-increase-productivity-the-ultimate-psychological-guide/

https://cognitiontoday.com/how-to-be-happy-8-ways-to-create-a-happy-life/

https://www.stress.org/workplace-stress

9 798858 922063 6